The Balancing Act

Recent decades have seen an increase in dual-income households. According to "The 2002 National Study of the Changing Workforce" conducted by the Families and Work Institute, 66 percent of American families were considered dual-earners in 1977. Dual-earners are defined as married couples working as salaried or wage employees. By 2002, the percentage of dual-earner families had risen to 78.

Not only are more of us working, but we are also working longer hours. Combined weekly work hours for dual-earning couples with children rose 10 hours per week during this period, from 81 hours in 1977 to 91 hours in 2002.

The Families and Work Institute's "When Work Works" project indicates that 67 percent of employed parents say they don't have enough time with their children, 63 percent say they don't have enough time with their spouses (up from 50 percent in 1992), and 55 percent say they don't have enough time for themselves.

This phenomenon is not unique to the United States; Sunil Joshi and others' article "Work-Life Balance: A Case of Social Responsibility or Competitive Advantage?" indicates that employees in the European Union are experiencing similar changes in their working lives and thus increases in stress levels.

Many factors are driving these changes, some of which include a desire for financial security in an increasingly insecure world and the rising costs of living. Another factor in these changes, according to Sunil Joshi and others, is that the role of work itself has changed from a matter of survival to a matter of personal satisfaction. People often work more to achieve success in their professional lives.

These fundamental and widespread changes in the working world have come with their share of challenges. Many of us have been forced to address work-life balance issues that were not as widespread in past generations, the most critical of which is how to manage multiple roles successfully—in our careers, within our families and relationships, and in other areas of our lives.

In the best of circumstances, these roles can complement each other to create a rich, fulfilling life. In most cases, however, we are struggling to keep up in one or more areas and often find that the roles are competing with each other. As a result, our stress levels rise, our mental and physical health is put at risk, and our relationships suffer. We tend to compensate by attempting to invest more time in each role, working *harder* rather than *smarter*, when we should consider how to spend our time more effectively and efficiently according to an overall work-life plan.

Given the challenges that are associated with attempting to balance all areas of our lives, the key question is: *How do I balance competing demands to ensure that I am spending my time most effectively in areas that are of value to me?* Ultimately, we have a number of aspirations in our lives and a limited amount of time in which to accomplish them.

The goals of this *Infoline* are to help you define what having a balanced life means and create a personalized work-life plan to enable you to stay on track despite ongoing, everyday challenges. Specifically, this *Infoline* will help you learn how to:

- identify your current and ongoing roles, or focus areas

- define your strategic objectives in each focus area

- develop tasks, actions, and communications to support each objective

- implement your work-life plan

- maintain and sustain an ideal quality of life.

The process of creating and implementing a work-life plan is truly an exercise in self-discovery and learning. The value you derive from this process depends on the effort you invest in it. With that in mind, let's get started.

Seeking an Alternative

At some point in your life, you may have felt as though your life was out of balance. There has likely been a time when you were devoting more energy in one area and neglecting other areas. Life may have felt like a juggling act, where you were doing just enough to get by for that moment, or for that day. However, sooner or later, it may have become obvious to you that other areas of your life were suffering and so, in turn, you focused on them. You may have felt more reactive than proactive. There was a constant back and forth—attention, then neglect—in several areas of your life. You may have felt like it was difficult to keep up, much less get ahead.

The differences between a life out of balance and a life in balance are easy to illustrate. Recall moments in your life when you have felt that your life is out of balance. Was it a struggle to get through each day? Did you feel disconnected from many areas of your life because you were focusing too much on only one area?

In contrast, recall a time when your life felt in balance. The various areas of your life felt harmonious and manageable. Your and others' expectations were consistent with your capabilities. Your actions supported specific goals, and you felt satisfied with your achievements. The feeling that your life is in balance does not happen by mere chance. To the contrary, feeling consistently in balance and self-directed is a result of deliberate, well-thought-out behavior, often the result of a carefully prepared and successfully implemented work-life plan.

When your life is "balanced," you feel as though the different areas of your life can co-exist, without feeling a sense of neglect in any one of them. You address your life proactively, as opposed to reactively. You have a plan and a set of goals for each area of your life, and your actions support those objectives. There is limited, if any, wasted energy. In addition, you successfully establish your personal expectations and others' expectations of you so you can manage, as much as possible, the demands being placed upon you.

The Purpose of a Work-Life Plan

You have probably experienced it on a relatively smaller scale: a sense of pride in knowing that your day went smoothly in large part because you gave thought to it before it arrived. Your actions for that day were linked to an overall plan, a plan with a purpose. The objective of a work-life plan is to take that same concept and apply it on a grander scale. Creating a work-life plan can help guide you personally and professionally to ensure that you are achieving true balance. A work-life plan is fundamental to the process of creating a balanced life.

In fact, most top athletes and business people have goals or objectives in place. Goals provide achievers with a long-term vision and short-term motivation. Defining goals is often more difficult than actually achieving them.

You may resist the idea of creating a plan for your life. You may view it as formalizing something that is best left up to fate. However, what does your experience tell you? Have your most significant achievements in life been the result of accidents or of deliberate, focused work? If you believe that no matter what you do, the outcome of a given situation is pre-determined, read the sidebar *Taking Charge of Life* at right to discover the benefits bestowed on people who choose to exercise control over the areas of their lives that they are capable of influencing. A work-life plan represents an aerial view that enables you to identify and compare activities that demand your time and energy.

The Components of a Work-Life Plan

A work-life plan is a comprehensive tool designed to assist you in visualizing, clarifying, and implementing a vision for your life. Although each person's work-life plan is unique, five related components are common to every work-life plan and maintenance process:

1. **Focus Areas.** These represent roles or functions within your life and can be personal or professional in nature. Each focus area comprises activities that support that focus area.

2. **Strategic Objectives.** For each focus area, there are numerous goals. You will prioritize these in order of what is most important to you.

Copyright © August 2004, *Infoline*, ASTD.

3. **Tasks, Actions, and Communications (TACs).** This component consists of the tactical steps or activities required to successfully achieve a particular strategic objective.

4. **Implementation Schedule.** The schedule defines a realistic timeline and approach for translating your vision into a reality.

5. **Work-Life Plan Maintenance.** This component relates to the ongoing evaluation and modification of your work-life plan.

The sidebar *The Work-Life Plan Development Process* illustrates how these components fit together.

Defining a Balanced Life

Before you create your plan for a balanced life, you need to understand what you want out of your professional and personal life and create your mission. Without these pieces, your life plan will lack a guiding force.

Understand What You Want

To realize your ideal, you need to understand what you want from life. Your vision should represent all that you aspire to, both personally and professionally. Close your eyes and take a few minutes to envision your ideal future. When formulating these thoughts, use your imagination and do not allow past experiences to discourage you from dreaming. Consider every wish or aspiration you have ever had. Think about how you want to develop as a professional. Consider what you have dreamed of achieving. Also think about personal goals and dreams, perhaps even ones that you entertained in childhood. Be open to any idea, any option. Use the questions in the sidebar *Envisioning Your Ideal Life* to help you start imagining the possibilities.

Now, capture these thoughts on paper using a brainstorming technique. Do not worry about being organized at this point, but be as specific as possible with your aspirations. The more detailed you are, the easier it will be to create clear steps to achieve your ideal life. For example, instead of "continue my education," you might want to say "earn my MBA in finance and graduate with top

Taking Charge of Life

What happens to people who take charge of their lives? Read some of the following examples to find out and then imagine what you can do.

Freedom

A case study in Patricia Pulliam Phillips's *In Action: Building a Successful Consulting Practice* describes a married couple who decided to leave their positions because of demands on their time and general workplace uncertainty to start their own consulting business. The husband describes the result in the following terms: "The past seven years have brought many challenges, but the greatest reward has been the freedom we have had to raise two kids and spend quality time together watching them grow. We keep sane hours, travel strategically, and make sure the business does not keep us from the most important things in life."

Harmony

Another case study in Linda Kyle Stromei's *In Action: Creating Mentoring and Coaching Programs* describes the effects of personal goal-setting on an instructional technologist's career and personal life. After just over a year of working with a personal coach, the subject of the case learned to balance her physical, emotional, and spiritual needs with her professional aims to achieve professional success as well as the flexibility, peace, and harmony she needed in her personal life. One lesson she learned in the process was "that needs aren't isolated; all is integrated."

Profit

In Darelyn "DJ" Mitsch's *In Action: Coaching for Extraordinary Results*, a case study reveals yet another potential benefit of balancing life priorities: profit! The subject of the case, Bob, who started his own construction company was in the beginning spending more and more time at work and getting fewer and fewer returns for the time. He recognized that both his professional and personal lives were heading toward a crisis, so he decided to work with a coach to balance his life. By letting go of some aspects of the job, focusing more on his strengths, and spending more time with his family, he was able to triple revenues and profits, achieve personal prosperity, and make huge strides toward financial independence.

The Work-Life Plan Development Process

The following flowchart illustrates the component activities of an ideal work-life plan. In the section about making your vision real, these activities and ways to carry them out are explained in greater detail.

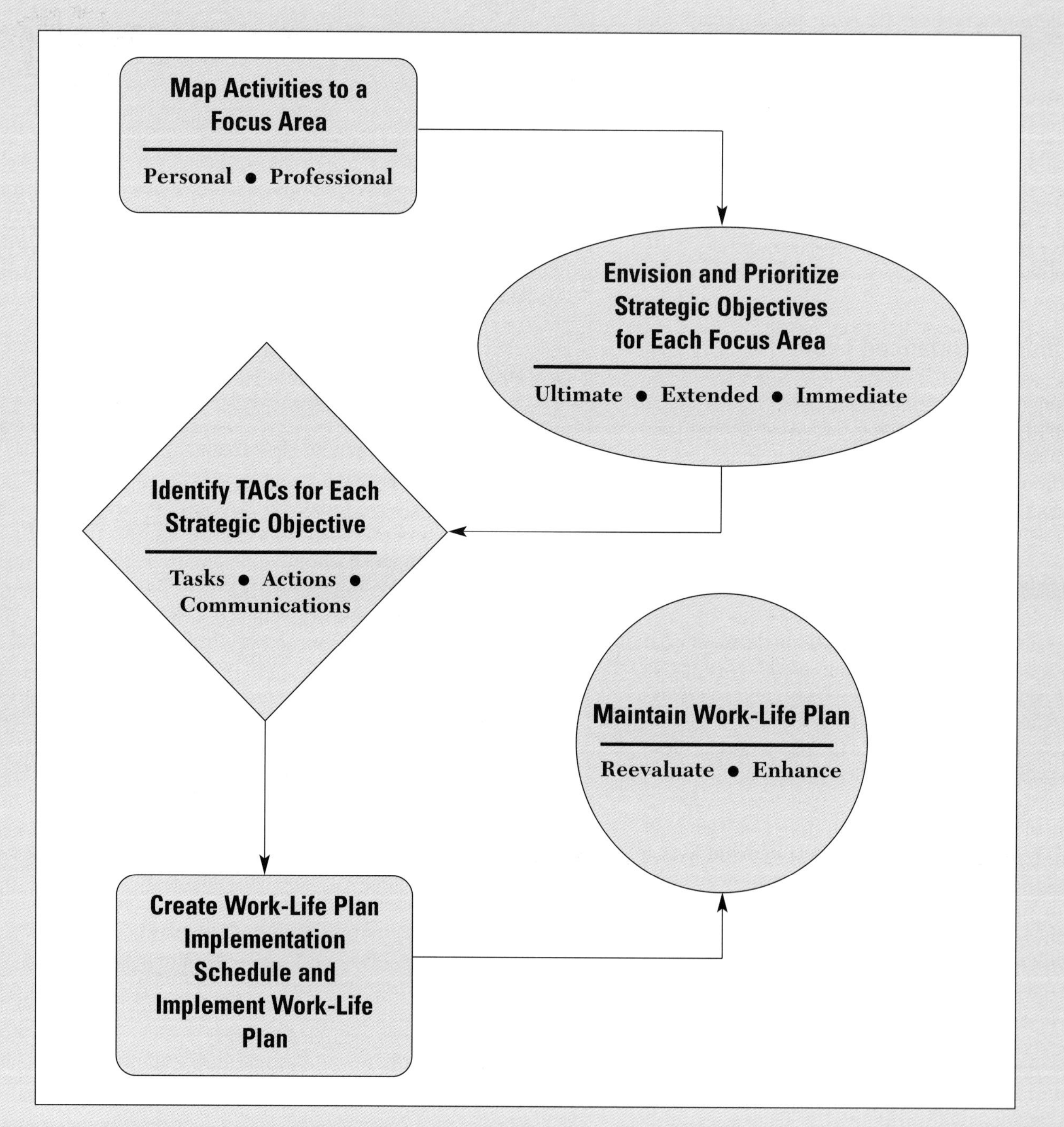

honors." This contemplative process requires you to be completely honest with yourself. Once you are finished, set the results of this brainstorming exercise aside. We will revisit them later.

Create Your Mission

Before you use the results from the previous brainstorming exercise, create a mission statement to prioritize your goals and shape your plan. Personal mission statements are helpful because they encapsulate what is of utmost importance to you and what inspires you. They reflect your values and your passions. To create a mission statement, answer the following questions:

- What purpose do I have in my life?

- What values do I want to represent?

- What actions am I taking to accomplish my purpose and adhere to my values?

- What am I learning to aid me in pursuing my goals?

A complete and purposeful mission statement can be as long as you require it to be to fully express your life mission. You should indicate what, generally speaking, you wish to accomplish and contribute at work and in life. You should also address the values or principles you wish to represent. Feel free to add an inspirational quotation at the end of your mission statement. See the sidebar *Personal Mission Statement* for an example.

Your personal mission statement should serve as an ongoing reminder of the person you aspire to be. Write down your mission statement and put it in a prominent place to ensure that you read it at least once daily. It will help keep your activities consistent with your goals. Remember that mission statements can change over time. Now that you have spent some time envisioning your ideal life and developing your mission statement, let's develop a road map to achieve that vision.

Making Your Vision Real

You have learned the purpose and components of a life plan, envisioned your ideal life, and created a mission statement. Now it's time to get to work on making your dream a reality. To achieve your vision, you will work through five steps:

1. Identify focus area activities.

2. Develop strategic objectives.

3. Identify TACs.

4. Develop an implementation schedule.

5. Maintain and update your life plan.

Step 1. Identify Focus Area Activities

To begin this process, group your activities, interests, and hobbies into a focus area. Focus areas are simply related activities that currently consume your time or are part of your life vision. People's focus areas are generally somewhat similar, but the way you define your goals within each focus area or your commitment to a particular focus area may be quite different from another person.

There are two categories of focus areas, personal and professional, and they are illustrated in the sidebar *Focus Areas*. Personal focus areas include:

- family, friends, and relationships
- physical and mental health
- intellectual development
- home maintenance
- community involvement
- spirituality.

Professional focus areas include:

- career management and development
- mentoring or grooming successors
- networking
- financial prosperity.

Envisioning Your Ideal Life

Think about the following questions to start brainstorming a vision of your ideal life. Be open to any idea, regardless of how impractical or unrealistic it may be. Also be honest with yourself; you may find that you do some things even though you don't really want to.

Family, Friends, and Relationships

- Who do you want to spend more time with?
- Who do you not want in your life?
- How would you like your relationships to be?
- What are you giving to others?
- What are you not giving to others?

Home Maintenance

- What would you like your home to look like?
- What is most important to you about your home?
- Does being at home make you feel relaxed and happy? Why or why not?

Physical and Mental Health

- What do you wish you could do, physically?
- What would you like your demeanor to be?
- What activities would you enjoy?
- What do you do for yourself that enhances your physical and mental well-being?

Community Involvement

- Do you feel you are contributing to the community?
- What volunteer opportunities would be meaningful?

Intellectual Development

- What activities are you enjoying?
- What are you learning?
- What would you like to learn?

Spirituality

- What kind of role would you like spirituality to play in your life? How can you achieve that?

Career Management and Development

- What does your career look like?
- What does your work schedule look like?
- Is your present position fulfilling? Why or why not?
- Have your professional interests and focus changed? Can your current position accommodate those changes?

Networking

- What opportunities do you have to network?
- What professional associations would you like to belong to?

Mentoring or Grooming Successors

- Who will be taking over your position as you advance?
- What are you teaching?

Financial Prosperity

- How much money would be "enough" for you?
- What are your financial goals?

Other

- How do your spend your evenings?
- How do you spend your weekends?
- How do you spend your vacations?

Using the job aid *Focus Area Mapping Sheet* at the end of this *Infoline,* map current and desired activities to focus areas. Use the results from your brainstorming exercise by mapping activities or pastimes to a focus area. For example, within the personal category, one focus area is physical and mental health. In this focus area, you might list sports you are active in (or desire to be active in) such as running, swimming, or yoga. You might also include goals related to diet and sleep in this focus area. Within the career management and development category, you might list tasks you regular engage in, such as doing research, designing training content, responding to emails, planning logistics, and so on. Also include activities that would further you in your professional goals. For example, if you wish to start your own consulting firm, you may need to spend more time networking and learning about marketing.

The goal of this process is to create an exhaustive list of all activities that currently consume, or will consume, your time and energy so you can begin to look at your time more realistically. If you have an activity that does not directly correspond to one of the focus areas listed on the worksheet, use the *Other* focus area at the end of the worksheet. Take time to complete this exercise, as it is the foundation of the work-life plan development process.

Step 2. Develop Strategic Objectives

Now that you have completed the focus area mapping process, the next step is to develop strategic objectives for each focus area. Strategic objectives are personalized and reasonable goals that are categorized as either ultimate (one year and beyond), extended (seven to 12 months), or immediate (one to six months). See the sidebar *Objectives Continuum* for an illustration.

Be sure that the goals you set are goals you would like to achieve, not what your employer or spouse wants you to do. To determine what your objectives are, review each focus area and think about the activities that you assigned to that focus area. In addition, refer to the results of your life vision brainstorming exercise and identify any specific objectives you may have listed there.

Personal Mission Statement

The following is an example of a well-crafted mission statement:

I will lead a life of honesty, self-direction, and fulfillment. I will learn relentlessly to bring more value to my trainees and my organization. I will be a devoted wife, a nurturing mother, a giving daughter, and a supportive sister. I will encourage my friends' pursuits and dreams and support them in every way I know how. I will lead a life of good health by preserving a strong and pure body and maintaining a healthful diet. I will continue to challenge my mind by exposing myself to new ideas and ways of thinking. Last, I will contribute to my community for the purpose of promoting peace and cooperation among all people.

"Go confidently in the direction of your dreams. Live the life you have imagined."—Henry David Thoreau

Use the job aid *Strategic Objectives and TACs Worksheet* at the end of this *Infoline* to document your objectives. Objectives should take the form of brief statements written in positive language (for example, "I want to . . ." or "I will . . ." as opposed to "Don't . . ."). Start with a single focus area and develop strategic objectives for that focus area.

For each objective, you also should note why it is a goal of yours. What value will you derive from meeting this objective? Take your time to complete this exercise. It could take days, or weeks, until you feel as though your strategic objectives are accurate and complete. Leave the priority and TACs sections blank at this point.

Once you have identified a specific goal, determine whether it falls into the ultimate, extended, or immediate category. It is usually easier to begin to define strategic objectives in the ultimate, or long-term, category and work backward from there. Ultimate goals can include anything you wish to achieve beyond the one-year timeframe. Ideally, incorporate some longer-term goals (for example, five to 10+ years) into your ultimate strategic objectives.

Focus Areas

The figure below illustrates the two major categories of focus groups: personal and professional. Note that focus areas can overlap between the two categories. In learning to realize your life vision, the first step is to identify activities within these focus groups that you engage in or want to engage in.

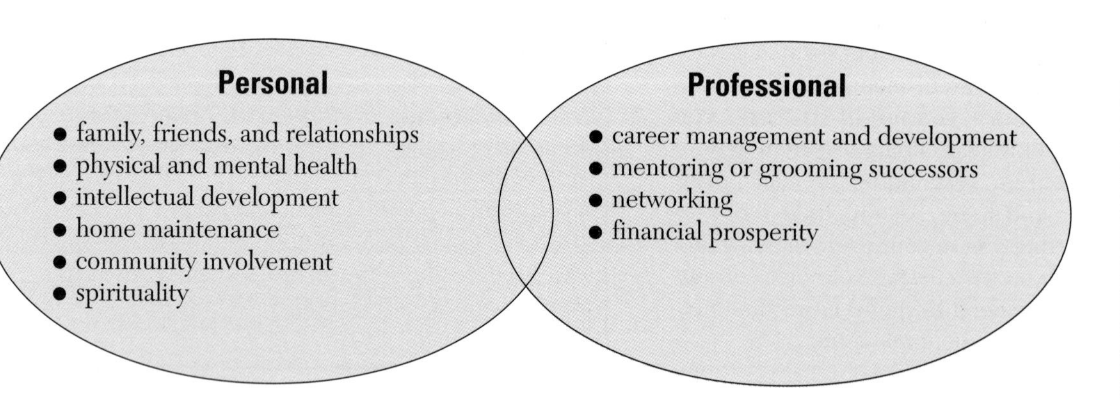

For example, within the physical and mental health focus area, one of your activities might be running. If you have long aspired to run a marathon, your immediate strategic objective might be to train by running three to six miles per day, five days per week, for the next six months. Your extended strategic objective might be to increase your mileage by running seven to 10 miles a day, five days per week and perhaps running in shorter competitive races. Another extended strategic objective would be to incorporate a 15-20 mile run at least once a week. Your ultimate goal would be to complete a marathon.

As much as possible, create supporting strategic objectives. For example, if you have an ultimate goal of being promoted to vice president of sales and marketing, you may want to set an extended goal of becoming a regional sales manager and an immediate goal of being the company's top performing sales representative.

Once you have identified your strategic objectives, you will need to determine the priority of each and assign target delivery dates. Prioritizing your objectives will enable you to spend your time more efficiently and effectively. To do this, ask yourself if the objective is time-sensitive, critical, or otherwise urgent and rate that objective higher than the others. In addition, there might be dependencies within your strategic objectives, or objectives that need to be accomplished before the others can begin or end. Use the *Strategic Objectives and TACs Worksheet* to review each of your strategic objective areas and prioritize the objectives within each of those areas using a relative scale (1-5, for example).

Once you have prioritized the objectives within each focus area, you can assign target delivery dates. Without deadlines, the work-life planning process can be frustrating. After all, in order to measure your progress you will need to define measurable goals. You can assign specific dates, weeks, months, or years, depending on the type of strategic objective (ultimate, extended, and immediate) and the nature of the goal. Be realistic when determining goals and assigning target dates. Do not aim too low, because achievement won't give you the sense of satisfaction you are aiming for. But don't aim unrealistically high either. That is a good way to fail and get no satisfaction from the process whatsoever. Again, take your time to complete this activity.

Note that striving for work-life balance is not unlike managing a project. If your workplace offers it, you may want to consider getting some project management training to help you accomplish your strategic objectives.

Step 3. Identify TACs

At this point you have identified strategic objectives for each focus area, grouped your objectives into the timeframes ultimate, extended, and immediate, and assigned target delivery dates to each of your objectives. Congratulations . . . you have just completed the most difficult part of this process!

Now, in order to achieve your objectives, you will need to create a list of tasks, actions, and communications (TACs). These TACs are the day-to-day activities required to achieve a goal. To continue the marathon training example, related TACs may include buying new running shoes and gear, joining a running club, scheduling recurring days or times to run each week, registering for shorter races, and registering for a marathon. Using the *Strategic Objectives and TACs Worksheet,* complete TACs for each of your focus areas at this time. Continue on a separate sheet of paper if you require additional space.

Step 4. Develop a Schedule

To realize your objectives, you must have a realistic tactical plan in place. Creating an implementation schedule requires assessing how you currently spend your time, reducing time spent on nonproductive activities (the sidebar *Time Robbers* presents a list of some common activities that may be taking more time than they need to), and focusing on accomplishing the TACs that relate to your strategic objectives.

Begin by going through your day and record how you spend your time for a few days. Be honest and realistic with yourself. When logging the time you spend on various tasks or activities, write down your estimate of the amount it will require. After tracking the way you use your time for a few days, review your log. Notice when your actions are aligned with your strategic objectives and when they are not. Also notice where your time estimates do not match reality and learn to adjust your time estimates appropriately.

In order to achieve your strategic objectives, you will need to dedicate time to performing TACs that are directly related to your goals. To accomplish this, eliminate as many activities as possible that do not relate to a specific strategic objective.

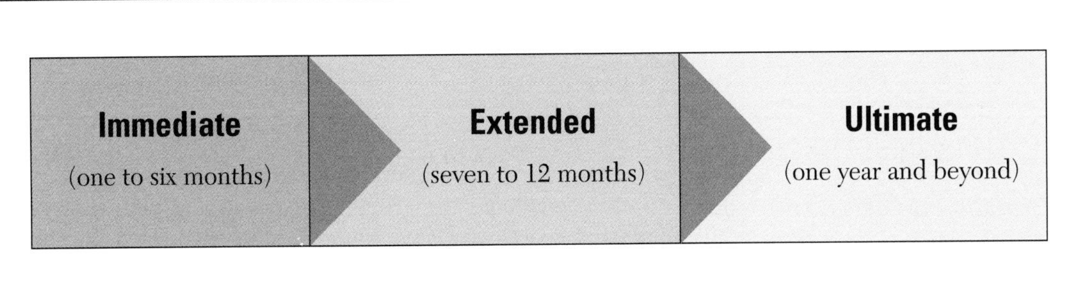

Objectives Continuum

After mapping your focus areas, you will want to develop strategic objectives for each focus area. Also categorize each objective or goal along the following continuum, which shows the timeframes "immediate," "extended," and "ultimate."

Time Robbers

Time robbers are a variety of things that eat up your time. In and of themselves, they may not be bad, but they often happen at the wrong time. Take a look at this list and see if your top three or four time robbers are here. Plan to eliminate or minimize the impact of these time robbers.

- travel
- conflicting priorities
- unrealistic time estimates
- lack of staff
- unclear goals
- television
- junk mail or email
- personal disorganization
- paperwork
- negative attitude
- nonessential reading
- poor planning
- waiting for answers or approval
- poor communication
- attempting to do too much
- lack of motivation
- civic activities
- games
- meetings
- equipment failures
- mistakes of others
- indecision
- socializing
- lack of delegation
- red tape
- lack of procedures
- peer demands
- lack of authority
- lack of self-discipline
- inability to say no
- procrastination
- interruptions
- over-involvement
- your mistakes
- failure to listen
- shifting priorities.

Adapted from Lenny T. Ralphs's "Basics of Time Management,"
Infoline *No. 259506.*

How do you eliminate low-value activities? You can choose to pull back your level of commitment or reestablish others' expectations of your commitment level. For example, if you are chairing a committee at work or within your community that is providing you with minimal value, you will need to communicate that you are reprioritizing your activities and no longer have 10 hours per week to donate to the cause.

You may also choose to delegate or hire out certain activities. If you do not enjoy mowing your lawn, and your financial situation allows for it, you may want to hire a mowing service, resulting in more available time for you on weekends. Also, let go of unhealthy or unfulfilling relationships that bring you down or discourage you from fulfilling your vision. Take this opportunity to break your bad habits and re-establish how you spend your time. The sidebar *Beyond Juggling* at right presents some other strategies for aligning your activities with your personal objectives.

Your workplace also may offer time and stress management training, which can help you identify ways to get more value from your activities. In addition, look into any work-life balance programs that your workplace offers, such as:

- flex time
- telecommuting
- childcare assistance
- family leave
- job-sharing programs
- employee assistance programs
- in-house services
- concierge services
- gym subsidies.

Consider finding out if you can change your work hours to accommodate your goals a bit better. Talk to your human resource department and find out what kinds of options you have.

It will not be possible to eliminate all activities that are out of alignment with your objectives. However, try to focus your time on areas that are of highest value to you and most aligned with your vision. Your goal is to be efficient and effective with your time and energy so that you may move closer to your vision each day.

Realize that the goal here is not to squeeze as many activities into as little time as possible. The objective is to spend more time doing activities that are meaningful to you and less time engaging in activities that are nonproductive or contradictory to your ultimate vision.

It will probably come as no surprise that this life-changing behavior will likely affect people close to you. Communicate the process you are going through with your family and closest friends. By doing so, you will not only proactively adjust their expectations of you and your commitment to certain focus areas, but you will probably gain their support. Better yet, they may even express an interest in following some of the same techniques that you have adopted for your life. Share the work-life plan development experience with others liberally. It is the best way for you to reinforce the process and continue to move toward your own vision.

After you have eliminated activities that are not aligned with your ultimate vision, start to work on TACs that *are* aligned with your strategic objectives. Concentrate on your ultimate strategic objectives within each of your focus areas and the associated TACs. Try to make progress in at least one area every day, even if you are only able to complete a very minor task or activity. Once you become more comfortable with this process and time permits, evaluate your extended and immediate objectives to ensure that you are actively taking steps toward those goals every week, as well.

If all of this seems too overwhelming to you, start by concentrating on a single focus area. Opt for the focus area that will yield the greatest effect or is most meaningful to you. Within this focus area, commit your time and energy to accomplishing a single immediate objective by completing the supporting TACs. Move slowly, but confidently. Once you have felt the satisfaction of completing one strategic objective, accomplish another. Before you know it, you may become addicted to focusing on your goals and achievements. The process itself is positively reinforcing: By completing one objective, you are compelled and motivated to complete another. Over time, you will become more confident in your ability to achieve goals, which will in turn encourage you to challenge yourself with more complex goals.

Beyond Juggling

In the *T+D* article "Beyond Juggling," Kathy Buckner and Kurt Sandholtz identify some strategies for realigning your activities with your goals:

Alternating

Alternaters want it all, but not all at once. Their work-life balance comes in separate, concentrated doses. They throw themselves into their careers with abandon, then cut way back or quit altogether to focus on their families or outside interests. This also can be done on a daily or weekly basis.

Outsourcing

Outsourcers achieve work-life balance by offloading responsibilities—usually in their personal lives—to free up time and energy for the tasks they care about most. Outsourcers with limited income rely on a robust, reciprocal network of family, friends, and neighbors.

Bundling

Bundlers involve themselves in fewer activities, but each activity fills more than one purpose. For example, a group of women meets three times a week to work out. They get physical exercise while deepening their relationships.

Techflexing

Techflexers use technology to liberate work hours from the rigid structure of a nine-to-five day, for example by telecommuting or connecting with family through cell phones and Web cams.

Simplifying

Simplifiers have decided they don't want it all. They've decided to commit less time and energy to nonessential activities both at work and at home. A common characteristic of simplifiers is to make certain sacrifices for greater freedom.

Adapted with permission from "Beyond Juggling," by Kathy Buckner and Kurt Sandholtz, T+D, *March 2003.*

Step 5. Maintain Your Work-Life Plan

To ensure that your daily activities directly support your goals, it is important that you set aside time every week to review your work-life plan. Allocate one hour at a regular time each week for a personal work-life plan review session. During this hour, you should:

- review and refine your focus areas

- revisit your ultimate, extended, and immediate strategic objectives and validate or set target delivery dates

- make adjustments, additions, or deletions as needed

- reflect on completed TACs and create a list of TACs to complete in the coming week

- ensure each of your TACs is *directly* aligned with one of your strategic objectives.

If you have achieved a goal easily, consider making your next objective slightly harder. If your time estimates were inaccurate, try to be more precise when determining a target delivery date. If, after achieving one objective, other objectives are affected, feel free to adjust or even remove the other goals from your work-life plan. If you discover a personal or professional weakness when achieving a goal, make sure you have an objective in place to improve on that weakness. Finally, reward yourself when you successfully achieve goals. In addition to the sense of accomplishment, tangible rewards are a valuable incentive.

Fulfilling Your Dreams

True dreamers never stop dreaming, nor do they ever cease achieving. As you achieve your objectives and become increasingly fulfilled in your life, you will continue to add strategic objectives to your work-life plan. Visions change and improve over time; embrace this change and remain confident in your abilities to achieve a uniquely remarkable quality of life.

This *Infoline* has provided you with the tools necessary to create an ideal work-life plan. You are now equipped to:

- create a vision and a mission to guide your life

- set immediate, extended, and ultimate strategic objectives within each of your focus areas

- develop TACs to support those objectives

- create and put into motion an implementation schedule to achieve your objectives

- maintain and evaluate your work-life plan and sustain a high quality of life.

As you continue to practice and hone these skills, continually commit yourself to achieving and maintaining your life vision. Living according to your ideal work-life plan is a unique expression of balance, self-direction, and fulfillment.

References & Resources

Articles

Abernathy, Donna, J. "A Get-Real Guide to Time Management." *Training & Development*, June 1999, pp. 22-26.

Allerton, Haidee E. "Blood, Sweat, and Cheers: Full Engagement." *T+D*, August 2003, pp. 34-41.

Booher, Dianna. "Unwind, Get a Life." *Training & Development*, September 1999, p. 60.

Buckner, Kathy, and Kurt Sandholtz. "Beyond Juggling." *T+D*, March 2003, pp. 68-70.

Crain's Chicago Business. "Balancing Work and Life." Special section, June 4, 2001, p. E1.

Families and Work Institute. "The 2002 National Study of the Changing Workforce." Available at http://www.familiesandwork.org.

———. "When Work Works." Available at http://www.familiesandwork.org.

Joshi, Sunil, and others. "Work-Life Balance: A Case of Social Responsibility or Competitive Advantage?" Available at http://www.worklifebalance.com/assets/pdfs/casestudy.pdf.

Koonce, Richard. "Practice Your Own Successful Habits." *Training & Development*, April 1999, pp. 48-53.

———. "There's More to Life Than Laptops." *Training & Development*, September 1999, pp. 42-45.

Kornbluh, Karen. "The Parent Trap." Available at http://www.newamericafoundation.org/index.cfm?pg=article&pubID=1152, 2003.

New America Foundation. "The American Family: Indicators of Economic Stress." Available at http://www.newamericafoundation.org/Download_Docs/pdfs/Pub_File_1381_1.pdf, 2003.

Silver, Cynthia. "Being There: The Time Dual-Earner Couples Spend With Their Children." *Canadian Social Trends,* Summer 2000.

Books

Covey, Stephen. *The 7 Habits of Highly Effective People.* New York: Simon & Shuster, 1989.

———. *First Things First: To Live, to Love, to Learn, to Leave a Legacy.* New York: Simon & Shuster, 1995.

Loehr, Jim, and Tony Schwartz. *The Power of Full Engagement.* New York: Free Press, 2003.

Merrill, A. Roger. *Life Matters: Creating a Dynamic Balance of Work, Family, Time, and Money.* New York: McGraw Hill, 2003.

Mitsch, Darelyn "DJ," ed. *In Action: Coaching for Extraordinary Results.* Alexandria, VA: ASTD, 2002.

Nippert-Eng, Christina E. *Home and Work: Negotiating Boundaries Through Everyday Life.* Chicago: University of Chicago Press, 1996.

Phillips, Patricia Pulliam, ed. *In Action: Building a Successful Consulting Practice.* Alexandria, VA: ASTD, 2002.

Sandholtz, Kurt, and others. *Beyond Juggling: Rebalancing Your Busy Life.* San Francisco: Berrett-Koehler, 2002.

Stromei, Linda Kyle, ed. *In Action: Creating Mentoring and Coaching Programs.* Alexandria, VA: ASTD, 2001.

Tracy, Brian. *Goals.* San Francisco: Berrett-Koehler, 2003.

Infolines

Ralphs, Lenny T. "Basics of Time Management." No. 259506.

Reitman, Annabelle. "Take Charge of Your Career." No. 250305.

Websites

www.familiesandwork.org

www.newamericafoundation.org

Job Aid

Focus Area Mapping Sheet

Identify the roles or functions in your life you currently participate in, or would like to participate in. Create an exhaustive list to gain a better understanding of how you spend your time. Use a separate sheet of paper if you need more room.

Personal Focus Areas

Family, Friends, and Relationships	Home Maintenance
1.	1.
2.	2.
3.	3.
4.	4.
5.	5.
Physical and Mental Health	Community Involvement
1.	1.
2.	2.
3.	3.
4.	4.
5.	5.
Intellectual Development	Spirituality
1.	1.
2.	2.
3.	3.
4.	4.
5.	5.

The material appearing on this page is not covered by copyright and may be reproduced at will.

Job Aid

Professional Focus Areas

Career Management and Development	Networking
1.	1.
2.	2.
3.	3.
4.	4.
5.	5.
Mentoring or Grooming Successors	Financial Prosperity
1.	1.
2.	2.
3.	3.
4.	4.
5.	5.
Other	
1.	
2.	
3.	
4.	
5.	
6.	
7.	
8.	
9.	

Job Aid

Strategic Objectives and TACs Worksheet

Identify strategic objectives and TACs for your focus areas. Copy the following worksheet and complete one per focus area.

Strategic Objectives	Priority
Ultimate (one year and beyond)	
Extended (seven to 12 months)	
Immediate (one to six months)	
Tasks, Actions, and Communications (TACs)